I0694958

The Artificial Brain
Volume 3

A Comical Look at Cognitive Dissonance

A Little Tree Food Forest Publication

Table of Contents

Introduction
A Not-So-Brave New World
of Brainy Deception

Welcome, dear readers, to a mind-bending journey through the wacky world of cognitive dissonance! Buckle up your brain cells, grab your sense of humor by the funny bone, and prepare for a ride that's wilder than a kangaroo on a pogo stick. In this fantastical adventure, we'll be diving headfirst into the swirling vortex where beliefs collide, reason takes a vacation, and our brains throw a party that even the most flamboyant peacock would find impressive.

Now, I know what you might be thinking (unless, of course, your brain has already decided to take a vacation): "What in the name of all things ridiculous is cognitive dissonance?" Well, dear reader, strap in, because we're about to unveil the grand circus that is your brain when it finds itself caught in a confounding tug of war between ideas.

Imagine, for a moment, that your mind is a carnival – a carnival filled

with popcorn-clutching clowns, acrobatic beliefs, and a ringmaster named Reason who occasionally takes a coffee break. Picture yourself strolling down the midway, past the cotton candy stand of Common Sense and the merry-go-round of Logic, until you stumble upon the main attraction: the Cognitive Dissonance Coaster. Yes, my friends, it's a ride that makes roller coasters look like sedentary recliners.

The Cognitive Dissonance Coaster, you see, doesn't follow the usual rules of theme park rides. It doesn't have a single trajectory or a predictable loop. Instead, it's a multi-dimensional, ever-shifting, upside-down-and-sideways whirlwind that can leave you both exhilarated and disoriented, much like a cat riding a Roomba. This coaster isn't made of steel tracks and wooden planks; it's constructed from the very fabric of your beliefs and the duct tape of your justifications. It's a ride where your brain's attempt to keep up with its own contradictions is akin to a squirrel trying to juggle flaming torches – entertaining to watch, but bound to end in fiery chaos.

So, what exactly is cognitive dissonance? It's that delightful sensation you experience when you find yourself, for instance, passionately arguing that chocolate is a vegetable (because cocoa comes from beans, duh) while simultaneously knowing that vegetables and desserts belong to separate food groups. It's the moment you proudly declare that you're a punctual person as you arrive late to your own time travel themed party. It's the reason you adamantly claim to be a cat person

even though your Instagram feed is 97% selfies with your dog.
In this book, we'll dissect the baffling behaviors that emerge when our brains enter the swirling waters of cognitive dissonance. We'll uncover the marvelous mechanisms that enable us to hold seemingly incompatible beliefs without the help of a magician's hat. We'll explore how this phenomenon is both a testament to our creativity and a reminder that our brains are as delightfully wonky as a unicycle with a flat tire.

But fear not, intrepid readers! This isn't a stuffy academic expedition through a land of jargon and footnotes. No, siree! We're here to learn and laugh, to prod at our own mental contradictions while wearing the clown noses of self-awareness. So, buckle up your funny bone, open your mind's parachute, and let's jump into the mirthful madness of cognitive dissonance. Remember, if your brain starts doing backflips of confusion, just go with the flow – because, hey, even a brain deserves a good laugh at its own expense!

Chapter 1
A Roller Coaster for the Mind
An Introduction to Cognitive Dissonance

Picture this: you're standing at the crossroads of Reason Avenue and Belief Boulevard, holding a map that's as reliable as a fortune cookie's advice on stock investments. On one hand, you've got your rock-solid convictions – the ones you proudly parade at family gatherings and defend with all the gusto of a knight protecting their chalice of truth. On the other hand, there's a niggling thought, a pesky voice whispering, "Maybe, just maybe, there's more to this than meets the eye."

Ladies and gentlemen, welcome to the perplexing realm of cognitive dissonance, where your brain's wrestling match with its own ideas could give the WWE a run for its money. Strap in, because we're about to embark on a ride that's equal parts enlightening and sidesplitting – a ride that's as unpredictable as a weather forecast in a land where meteorology is based on tarot card readings.

The Confused Brain Dance
When Beliefs Clash and Create Chaos

Picture a dance floor. It's a pulsating kaleidoscope of thoughts and feelings, and your beliefs are the waltzing partners, elegantly twirling in their sequined gowns of conviction. You're watching this mesmerizing performance from the balcony of your conscious mind, when suddenly, out of nowhere, an unexpected guest crashes the party: an opposing belief, wearing a tutu of doubt and tap dancing like there's no tomorrow.

At first, your beliefs stare at each other like rival ballerinas competing for the lead role in "Swan Lake." There's tension in the air, like the palpable awkwardness of being caught wearing mismatched socks at a black-tie event. This, my friends, is the inception of cognitive dissonance – a mental state where your brain finds itself juggling two contradictory beliefs, and it's as bewildering as discovering your pet goldfish has been ghostwriting Shakespearean sonnets.

Cognitive Dissonance: Where Logic Takes a
Backflip and Reality Hides in the Closet

Imagine you're in a reality TV show, "Brain Survivor," where your beliefs are the contestants competing in a series of twisted challenges. The prize? A trophy made of pure rationality and the chance to prove that yes, you can totally believe in the existence of time-traveling hamsters without batting an eyelash.

Cognitive dissonance is the sneaky twist the show's producers throw in to stir the pot. Contestants, get ready to face the absurdity of your convictions! Suddenly, you're faced with undeniable evidence that hamsters are, in fact, not time travelers but just tiny furballs with a penchant for exercise wheels. Your brain, however, is in a tight spot. It's like watching a magician reveal the secret behind a mind-blowing trick – you desperately want to believe in the magic, even though the rabbit was definitely not pulled out of an alternate dimension.

The Comedic Tragedy: Why Your Brain Can't Handle Its Own Contradictions

Let's talk about your brain for a moment. It's a marvelous organ, capable of composing symphonies, decoding hieroglyphics, and reciting the entire lyrics of the Macarena (hey, we all have our talents). But when it comes to managing contradictions, your brain starts to resemble a circus juggler who's trying to balance an elephant, a toaster, and a flaming bowling pin.

Why, oh why, does your brain struggle with these conflicting beliefs? Well, consider this: your brain is like a control center staffed by a diverse group of opinionated bureaucrats. Each belief is represented by a different bureaucrat, and when they're faced with contradictions, they bicker and squabble like preschoolers fighting over the last cookie. Meanwhile, your brain's CEO, Reason, is on vacation, leaving the interns of Impulse and Emotion to referee the chaos.

In this topsy-turvy comedy of errors, cognitive dissonance takes center stage, serving as the punchline to a cosmic joke. It's as if your brain decided to throw a party, inviting the Queen of Logic and the Court Jester of Nonsense, and then realized it forgot to order the party favors. And so, as the night unfolds, your brain waltzes through a merry dance of justifications, absurd rationalizations, and a chorus line of "I totally meant to do that" explanations.

Ladies and gentlemen, welcome to the opening act of our circus of the mind. The Cognitive Dissonance Coaster is just revving up, and in the chapters to come, we'll dive deeper into this delightful labyrinth of contradictory beliefs, uncover the secret sauce behind justifying the unjustifiable, and explore how we navigate the carnival of our own quirky thoughts. So, keep your hands and feet inside the ride at all times, and let's revel in the absurdity of our own brain's greatest comedy show!

Chapter 2
The Great Balancing Act
Juggling Beliefs and Reality

Ahoy, fellow travelers of the mind! As we continue our uproarious expedition into the perplexing realm of cognitive dissonance, let's take a moment to appreciate the sheer audacity of our brains attempting to juggle beliefs that seem about as compatible as a cat and a bubble bath. Welcome to the Great Balancing Act, where our mental gymnasts flex their cognitive muscles and attempt feats of flexibility that would make a contortionist raise an impressed eyebrow.

Tightrope Walking with Thoughts
How We Trick Ourselves into Believing the Unbelievable
Imagine yourself walking a tightrope suspended high above a sea of contradicting thoughts, much like a squirrel prancing along an electrical wire while considering its career options. On one side, you have the belief that chocolate cake is a legitimate breakfast item – after all, cocoa does come from a bean, doesn't it? On the other side, there's

the knowledge that a breakfast should ideally consist of more nutrients than a toddler's crayon collection.

As you tiptoe along this mental tightrope, your brain pulls out all the stops to maintain equilibrium. It's a spectacle that would make circus lions look like well-behaved house cats. Your brain employs a fancy footwork technique called "selective attention," which is essentially your inner bouncer tossing out any thoughts that threaten to disrupt the harmonious dance of your beliefs. This way, you can strut your stuff on the tightrope of rationalization without tripping over the inconvenient truth that cake for breakfast might not be a brilliant life choice.

The Olympic Sport of Mental Gymnastics
Practicing the Art of Justification

Let's be honest – the mental gymnastics we perform to avoid the discomfort of cognitive dissonance could earn us gold medals in the "Self-Deception Olympics." Have you ever found yourself justifying your impulse purchase of a life-sized rubber duck by proclaiming that it's an essential item for "emergency bath time entertainment"? Congratulations, you're a contender for the mental gymnastics hall of fame!

In this grand spectacle, our brains leap, twist, and somersault through a series of elaborate routines that would make Olympic gymnast give

a standing ovation. Imagine you're watching an athlete gracefully maneuver through a routine of "explaining how you really, really needed that third slice of pizza." With a disarming smile, they twist their logic into pretzels, execute a perfect pirouette of "well, I did run up the stairs today," and stick the landing with a triple-flip declaration of "it's all about balance, you know?"

The Bizarre Power of Justifying Ice Cream for Breakfast A Case Study in Delicious Rationalization

Let's dive into a case study that will put our newfound knowledge of cognitive dissonance to the test. Meet Jane, a self-proclaimed ice cream enthusiast who has just finished an entire pint of rocky road before the roosters have even considered crowing. Now, Jane could experience a slight hiccup in her brain as it realizes that ice cream isn't exactly a recommended breakfast food group.

However, Jane's brain doesn't panic; it revs up its rationalization engines. "Well," it chirps, "calcium is good for bones, and ice cream has milk, which has calcium, so technically I'm building strong bones while satisfying my sweet tooth." And there you have it, folks – the art of turning a dessert indulgence into a health-conscious decision. Jane's brain has executed a perfect triple axel of justification, leaving the judges (that's us) both amused and somewhat impressed.

Ladies and gentlemen, as we twirl our way through the realm

of justifications and mental gymnastics, we come to a profound realization: our brains are like master illusionists, capable of turning a mundane explanation into a spectacle worthy of a Vegas stage. So, let's raise our mental pom-poms and give a round of applause to the acrobats within our minds who balance beliefs with all the finesse of a squirrel balancing a nut on its nose.

In the chapters to come, we'll venture further into the zany world of cognitive dissonance, exploring how it shapes our everyday decisions, our relationships with reality, and the hilarious masquerade ball that is our self-image. Get ready for a wild ride, folks, because the circus tent is still standing, and the Cognitive Dissonance Coaster is revving up for more antics!

Chapter 3
A Symphony of Silliness
Cognitive Dissonance in Everyday Life

Greetings, fellow cosmic comedians! As we march on through the hall of mirrors that is our own minds, it's time to delve into the vibrant tapestry of cognitive dissonance in the theater of everyday life. From wardrobe wars to political absurdities, get ready to witness a symphony of silliness that could give a circus orchestra a run for its kazoo money. So, grab your popcorn and your most elastic pair of logic-defying suspenders – we're about to explore how cognitive dissonance turns the mundane into the marvelously hilarious.

Wardrobe Wars: Why Your Closet Is a Battleground of Fashion and Identity

Imagine stepping into your closet and staring at the bewildering chaos of clothing choices. On one hand, there's the vintage prom dress you haven't worn in a decade, yet you're convinced that you'll wear it to the grocery store one day – you know, just in case the frozen food aisle turns into a ballroom dance floor. On the other hand, there's your collection of worn-out T-shirts, each one commemorating a concert you didn't attend but desperately want to be associated with.

Enter cognitive dissonance, stage left. It's like having a sartorial debate with a thousand versions of yourself. Your inner fashionista is screaming, "You can totally pull off leather pants, even in a corporate meeting!" while your inner comfort-seeker is gently suggesting, "Sweatpants are the true champions of freedom, my friend."
And so, you venture out into the world, confidently sporting a mismatched ensemble that shouts, "I'm eclectic!" while quietly muttering, "I'm just too lazy to do laundry." Congratulations – you've just orchestrated a wardrobe symphony that would make Beethoven's Fifth sound like a kazoo quartet.

The "I'm on a Diet" Paradox: How Salads and Fries Coexist in the Minds of the Strong-Willed

Ah, the age-old battle between your desire to eat healthier and your unwavering love for all things deep-fried and dripping in cheese.

You're at a restaurant, and there it is – the salad menu, beckoning like a choir of angelic dietitians. But then, from the corner of your eye, you spot the burger and fries combo, and suddenly, your inner angel is replaced by a devil wearing a napkin as a bib.

As you agonize over the menu, your brain is running a marathon, sprinting between the finish line of self-control and the enticing aroma of comfort food. It's a dilemma worthy of Shakespearean tragedy – to eat or not to eat, that is the question. The solution? The "I'll have a salad but with extra bacon" compromise, a feat of culinary acrobatics that would leave world-renowned chefs both impressed and horrified.

Politics and Peculiarities
Exploring the Mind-Bending Feats of Political Supporters

Ah, the realm of politics – where cognitive dissonance dons its fanciest attire and does the cha-cha with your convictions. Imagine being a die-hard supporter of a candidate whose policies are as clear as a foggy window, yet you're convinced they're the savior of mankind. Your brain becomes a contortionist, bending and twisting your beliefs until they're as convoluted as a pretzel in a funhouse mirror.

As you engage in heated debates, your arguments resemble a circus performance, complete with lion-taming acts and acrobats doing backflips to avoid acknowledging the glaring inconsistencies in your candidate's platform. It's like watching a magician perform a disappearing act with your critical thinking skills, leaving you both bewildered and thoroughly entertained.

Ladies and gentlemen, as we navigate the carnival of cognitive dissonance in our everyday lives, let's remember that we're all players in this grand comedic theater. From the hilarious clothing choices that define us to the bellyaches caused by our love-hate relationship with French fries, our quirks and contradictions are what make us human, relatable, and infinitely amusing. So, grab your conductor's baton and join the orchestra of life's silliness as we continue our symphonic exploration of the world through the lens of cognitive dissonance.

The show must go on, my friends, and we're all stars in this glorious, uproarious production!

Chapter 4
From Flat Earth to Moon Cheese
The Spectrum of Cognitive Dissonance

Greetings, intrepid explorers of the absurd! As we journey deeper into the rabbit hole of cognitive dissonance, prepare to be dazzled by the mind-bending kaleidoscope of beliefs that span the spectrum from the mildly curious to the downright outrageous. From unicorns to conspiracy theories, buckle up, because we're about to venture into the fantastical realm where reality and imagination engage in a wild tango.

Believing in Unicorns: When Nonsensical Ideas Find Shelter in Stubborn Minds

Ah, the unicorn – that mythical creature of legend, known for its majestic appearance, sparkly demeanor, and complete absence from the fossil record. Yet, in the vast expanse of human imagination, there are those who ardently believe that these horned equines trot merrily around somewhere, possibly sipping chai lattes and engaging in deep conversations about the merits of glitter.

Cue cognitive dissonance, prancing onto the scene with all the grace of a tap-dancing elephant. On one hand, you have the pile of evidence suggesting that unicorns are more elusive than a two-year-old sharing candy. On the other hand, you've got the die-hard unicorn enthusiast who insists that they've seen one in their neighbor's petting zoo.

So, how does one reconcile this fantastical belief with the reality of the animal kingdom? Simple – with a dash of magical thinking and a sprinkle of cognitive dissonance. After all, if your brain can justify eating a tub of ice cream for emotional support, it can surely find a way to make room for a rainbow-maned, horned horse in the grand pantheon of mythical creatures.

Conspiracy Theories: The Art of Turning Tin Foil Hats into Fashion Statements

Ah, conspiracy theories – the gold mines of cognitive dissonance, where the rational meets the eccentric and the plausible gives way to the preposterous. From moon landings being staged on a Hollywood set to lizard people secretly controlling world governments, the conspiracy buffet offers a smorgasbord of ideas that can make even the most elaborate spaghetti dish look like a snack.

Picture this: you're chatting with a friend who claims that Elvis Presley faked his death to become an undercover FBI agent. Your brain, not quite sure whether to salute or laugh, wobbles on a tightrope of

disbelief. But your friend, fueled by the power of cognitive dissonance, stands firm, resolute in their conviction that the King of Rock 'n' Roll moonlights as a G-man.

In the grand theater of conspiracy theories, cognitive dissonance takes on the role of the lead actor, delivering monologues that weave a tangled web of intrigue and hilarity. As we watch the drama unfold, we can't help but marvel at the human capacity to embrace the outlandish while donning a tin foil hat with pride.

When Aliens and Garden Gnomes Collide
Navigating the Landscape of Fantastical Beliefs
As we tiptoe along the spectrum of cognitive dissonance, we encounter a bizarre crossroads where aliens mingle with garden gnomes, Bigfoot serves tea to the Loch Ness Monster, and reality itself throws up its hands in surrender. Imagine a world where believers in extraterrestrial life argue passionately that they've been personally abducted, while skeptics insist that their neighbor's unusually tall shadow is definitely a sasquatch.

In this whimsical carnival of beliefs, cognitive dissonance waltzes between the whimsical and the weird, orchestrating a symphony that's as puzzling as a jigsaw puzzle missing half its pieces. As we observe the cosmic dance between our convictions and the implausible, let's not forget that it's the sheer diversity of our thoughts that makes life a ceaselessly entertaining, endlessly perplexing adventure.

Ladies and gentlemen, as we continue our odyssey through cognitive dissonance, remember that while the spectrum of beliefs may stretch from the rational to the fantastical, the laughter that arises from our embrace of the absurd is universal. So, put on your mental snorkel and dive into the sea of imagination, where dolphins may or may not communicate in Klingon, and where the depths of human belief are as boundless as the cosmos itself. The journey is wild, my friends, but the entertainment is truly out of this world!

Chapter 5
Mind Games and Mental Acrobatics
Unveiling the Mechanisms

Ahoy, my fellow mental contortionists! As we venture into the heart of cognitive dissonance, it's time to put on our thinking caps and examine the perplexing mechanisms that drive this grand circus of the mind. From selective ignorance to echo chambers, get ready to peel back the curtain and uncover the nuts and bolts of our brain's most entertaining acrobatics.

Selective Ignorance 101: How to Ignore Mountains of Evidence with a Straight Face

Imagine you're hosting a dinner party where the main course is a mountain of broccoli, and your guests are ardent vegetable haters. Now, you could present a feast of research explaining the health benefits of greens, but instead, you opt for the path of selective ignorance. You serve the broccoli with a flourish, declaring, "It's just like eating tiny trees, and who doesn't love a good forest?"

Cue cognitive dissonance, wearing a blindfold and tap-dancing through the room. On one hand, there's a pile of scientific studies attesting to the nutritional wonders of broccoli. On the other hand, there's your belief that vegetables are the sworn enemy of taste buds everywhere. So, you tango your way into a state of selective ignorance, acknowledging the existence of evidence while politely declining its invitation to your dinner table.

The Echo Chamber Orchestra: Surrounding Yourself with Applause for Every Tune You Play

Welcome to the Echo Chamber Orchestra, where the sweet melodies of affirmation resonate with the perfect pitch of self-assurance. Imagine a room filled with people who applaud your every statement, regardless of how nonsensical it may be. "I've invented a time machine," you declare, and the audience bursts into applause, completely ignoring the lack of any time-traveling vehicles in sight.

Cue cognitive dissonance, conducting an orchestra of validation with all the gusto of a maestro leading a symphony. On one hand, there's the chorus of rational thought, questioning the feasibility of time travel. On the other hand, there's the intoxicating melody of applause, validating your every whimsical notion. Your brain orchestrates a harmonious duet between these conflicting forces, creating a blissful tune that's equal parts amusing and delusional.

Flimsy Pillars and House of Cards: Why Constructing Arguments Is Like Building with Marshmallows

Imagine constructing an argument as if you're building a house of cards – a house that's as sturdy as a Jenga tower made of jellybeans. You start with a foundation of conviction, stack on some anecdotal evidence, and crown it all with a cherry-picked statistic. Voilà! Your argument stands tall, ready to withstand any gust of reason. Or does it?

Cue cognitive dissonance, armed with a gusty breeze of skepticism. On one hand, there's the fragile structure of your argument, which could collapse faster than a soufflé during an earthquake. On the other hand, there's your belief in the ironclad nature of your logic, a belief as unshakeable as a tree during a gentle summer breeze.

And so, the dance of cognitive dissonance continues – a duet of flimsy pillars and delicate cards, executed with the finesse of a ballerina tiptoeing through a field of dandelions. As we unravel the intricacies of constructing arguments in the grand circus of our minds, let's remember that while our logical edifices might resemble a house of cards, the laughter that springs forth from our own folly is as solid as the foundation of human nature itself.

Ladies and gentlemen, as we peel back the layers of cognitive dissonance's inner workings, let's embrace the whimsy and wonder of our mental acrobatics. From selective ignorance to echo chambers, from flimsy arguments to well-meaning self-delusion, these mechanisms remind us that our brains are like magicians, capable of turning mere thoughts into fantastical performances that leave us both amused and baffled. So, grab your mental trapeze, summon your inner daredevil, and let's soar through the sky of understanding, navigating the thrilling loop-de-loops of cognitive dissonance's mechanical marvels!

Chapter 6
Breaking the Comedy Cycle
Strategies for Taming Cognitive Dissonance

Greetings, fellow dissonance detectives! As we journey further into the wild landscape of our own minds, it's time to don our detective hats, monocles, and a healthy dose of self-awareness. In this chapter, we'll delve into the art of breaking the comedy cycle of cognitive dissonance – a process that's as tricky as teaching a cat to play the saxophone. So, buckle up, my friends, because we're about to embark on a quest to transform our mental gymnastics into a graceful ballet.

The Mirror of Self-Reflection: Gazing at Your Own Contradictions and Bursting into Laughter

Imagine standing in front of a magic mirror that reflects not your physical form, but your inner contradictions and hilariously implausible justifications. As you gaze into this mirror, you see yourself explaining to a crowd why wearing socks with sandals is actually a groundbreaking fashion statement, while your reflection raises an eyebrow of disbelief.

Cue cognitive dissonance, sashaying into view with a bouquet of roses and a confetti cannon. On one hand, there's your performance of justifying the unjustifiable, complete with logical loopholes and rhetorical flourishes. On the other hand, there's the mirror's merciless reflection, exposing the absurdity of your contorted arguments.

As you peer into this mirror, you're reminded that self-awareness is the jester's jest, the ultimate punchline to your brain's cosmic comedy routine. Laughter bubbles forth as you embrace the sheer silliness of your mental acrobatics, and suddenly, you're both the comedian and the audience, the joke teller and the one doubled over with laughter.

The Art of Humble Pie
Learning to Admit You Were Wrong Without Imploding

Ah, the taste of humble pie – a dish served with a side of humility and a dollop of cognitive dissonance. Imagine finding yourself in a situation where you realize that your once-firm belief in the existence of talking dolphins might not hold water (pun intended). You're faced with a crossroads: continue clinging to your implausible convictions or dive headfirst into the ocean of reality.

Cue cognitive dissonance, donning a snorkel and flippers as it takes you on a deep-sea expedition of self-discovery. On one hand,

there's your reluctance to admit that maybe, just maybe, dolphins communicate more through clicks than Shakespearean sonnets. On the other hand, there's the siren call of reason, beckoning you to embrace the waves of new information.

As you nibble on a slice of humble pie, you find that cognitive dissonance is like a wise old mentor, teaching you that the act of admitting you were wrong doesn't result in the sky falling or the earth quaking. In fact, it's the key to freeing yourself from the straitjacket of self-imposed absurdities and opening the door to personal growth and discovery.

Cognitive Flexibility
The Jedi Mind Trick for Balancing Beliefs and Reality

Imagine yourself as a cognitive Jedi, armed not with a lightsaber but with a Jedi mind trick that can bend your thoughts like a pretzel. You stand in the midst of conflicting beliefs, poised to use your cognitive flexibility to perform a mental magic trick that leaves everyone scratching their heads in wonder.

Cue cognitive dissonance, dressed as Yoda and wielding the wisdom of ages. On one hand, there's your belief that marshmallows are vegetables (because they come from plants, right?). On the other hand, there's the reality that marshmallows are essentially sugar and air. And so, you deploy your Jedi mind trick, reshaping your perspective until marshmallows become a symbol of levity rather than a source of nutritional confusion.

In this grand cosmic circus of cognitive flexibility, you realize that it's not about bending your beliefs to fit reality, but rather finding the sweet spot where your beliefs and reality engage in a harmonious tango. It's a dance that requires nimble steps, a good sense of humor, and a willingness to embrace the ever-evolving nature of your thoughts.

Ladies and gentlemen, as we navigate the labyrinth of cognitive dissonance with the grace of circus performers, let's remember that the art of breaking the comedy cycle is not about eradicating absurdity from our minds, but rather celebrating the joyous dance of contradictions that makes us human. So, don your mental ballet shoes, strike up the orchestra of self-reflection, and let's pirouette through the world of cognitive dissonance, turning our inner jesters into philosophers and our comedy into wisdom. The stage is set, my friends, and the laughter is our greatest encore!

Chapter 7
Navigating the Funhouse
Embracing the Laughter in Our Own Minds

Ahoy, my merry mariners of mirth! As we approach the grand finale of our escapade into the world of cognitive dissonance, it's time to step into the funhouse of our minds, where laughter echoes off the walls of absurdity and our thoughts become the amusement park of the imagination. From the joy of self-acceptance to the thrill of embracing contradictions, get ready for a roller coaster of hilarity that leaves your sides aching and your heart soaring.

Tickling Your Inner Funny Bone
Laughter as a Bridge to Self-Acceptance
Imagine your inner critic as a stand-up comedian performing a routine filled with self-deprecating jokes about your quirks, idiosyncrasies, and questionable life choices. As you listen, you find yourself laughing not out of embarrassment, but out of genuine amusement at the comedic masterpiece that is your own life.

Cue cognitive dissonance, arriving on the scene like a mischievous sprite, armed with a whoopee cushion and a clown wig. On one hand, there's the voice that chastises you for your eccentricities. On the other hand, there's the realization that these quirks are what make you wonderfully, uniquely, and unabashedly you.

In this sidesplitting circus of self-acceptance, cognitive dissonance becomes your very own stand-up comedian, delivering punchlines that celebrate your contradictions and quirks. And as you laugh uproariously at the absurdity of your own existence, you realize that the key to embracing your true self is not in silencing the critic, but in inviting the jester to take center stage.

Carnival of Contradictions
Finding Harmony in the Comedy of Beliefs

Imagine strolling through a carnival where each attraction is a manifestation of your own beliefs – the dunk tank of "Ice Cream for Breakfast," the roller coaster of "Unicorns and Moon Cheese," and the mirror maze of "Wardrobe Wars." As you navigate this carnival of contradictions, you discover that the laughter of self-awareness is the soundtrack that ties it all together.

Cue cognitive dissonance, dressed as a ringleader with a top hat and a booming voice. On one hand, there's the belief that you must adhere to a single, consistent narrative. On the other hand, there's the realization

that life's greatest comedy emerges from the collision of beliefs and the orchestration of the unexpected.

In this grand carnival of contradictions, cognitive dissonance leads the parade, reminding you that life's greatest adventure is not in seeking rigid consistency, but in embracing the ever-changing landscape of your thoughts. The laughter that resonates through the carnival becomes a celebration of the human spirit – whimsical, unpredictable, and delightfully contradictory.

The Cosmic Punchline
Embracing the Humor in Our Beautiful Messiness
Imagine the universe as a cosmic joke, with stars and galaxies as the setup and your bewildering thoughts as the punchline. As you contemplate the absurdity of existence, you find that the more you lean into the humor, the more the universe seems to respond with twinkling stars of understanding.

Cue cognitive dissonance, adorned in celestial attire, offering you a cosmic telescope to view your life's tapestry of contradictions. On one hand, there's the desire to unravel life's mysteries. On the other hand, there's the joy of embracing the beautiful messiness of it all.

In this celestial comedy of existence, cognitive dissonance becomes your guide to navigating the constellations of belief, leading you to the heart of understanding where laughter and wisdom intertwine. And as you gaze upon the night sky of your own mind, you're reminded that life's greatest lessons are often hidden in the folds of its most hilarious moments.

Ladies and gentlemen, as we bid farewell to the circus of cognitive dissonance, let's remember that life is a grand comedy show – one where our beliefs and contradictions dance together in harmony, one where laughter becomes the balm that heals the soul. So, put on your cosmic spectacles, step into the funhouse of your mind, and let's celebrate the magnificent tapestry of thoughts that make us the star performers in the greatest show on Earth. The curtain may fall, my friends, but the laughter echoes on forever!

Chapter 8
The Curtain Call
A Standing Ovation for the Absurdity of Being Human

Ladies and gentlemen, clowns and jesters, skeptics and believers – the time has come for our grand finale, the curtain call of our journey through the delightful realm of cognitive dissonance. As we take our bows and soak in the laughter, let's reflect on the lessons learned, the chuckles shared, and the wisdom gained from embracing the whimsy of our own minds.

The Standing Ovation of Imperfection
Celebrating the Comedy of Being Human

Imagine a theater filled with an enthusiastic audience, each person applauding not for a flawless performance, but for the sheer joy of witnessing the wonderful messiness of the human experience. The spotlight shines on you, the star of the show, with all your quirks and contradictions on full display. The applause is not just for your successes, but for your courage to stumble, your willingness to embrace your cognitive gymnastics, and your ability to find humor even in the face of your own absurdities.

Cue cognitive dissonance, dressed as the conductor of this grand symphony, orchestrating the applause and laughter that resonate through the auditorium. On one hand, there's the desire for perfection, the notion that every thought should be polished and pristine. On the other hand, there's the recognition that it's our imperfections, our contradictions, and our ability to laugh at ourselves that truly define our humanity.

As the final notes of the symphony of cognitive dissonance ring out, you stand on the stage of your own mind, basking in the glow of acceptance and understanding. The standing ovation you receive is not just from the imaginary audience, but from the depths of your own heart, celebrating the marvelous, hilarious, and awe-inspiring journey of being human.

The Wisdom in Laughter
Unearthing the Hidden Nuggets of Truth

Imagine a treasure chest filled with sparkling jewels of wisdom, buried beneath layers of laughter and absurdity. As you unlock the chest, you discover that the gems are not just polished truths, but the raw and uncut insights that emerge when you allow your beliefs to collide and

dance in the spotlight of your consciousness.

Cue cognitive dissonance, now dressed as a treasure hunter, guiding you through the process of unearthing these gems. On one hand, there's the temptation to seek answers that are neat and tidy. On the other hand, there's the realization that it's in the messiness, the contradictions, and the unexpected laughter that the most profound wisdom resides.

In this treasure hunt of the mind, cognitive dissonance becomes your guide, leading you through the labyrinth of thoughts to the heart of understanding. And as you examine each glittering gem, you recognize that wisdom is not just found in the answers, but in the questions, the uncertainties, and the willingness to explore the vast expanse of your own thoughts.

Curtain Call and New Beginnings
The Ongoing Comedy of Growth

As the curtain falls on our exploration of cognitive dissonance, let's remember that this is not the end, but a new beginning. The circus of the mind continues, the laughter echoes on, and the grand comedy of growth never ceases its performance.

Cue cognitive dissonance, now standing beside you, ready to embark on new adventures. On one hand, there's the sense of completion, the knowledge that you've navigated the realm of contradictions. On the other hand, there's the excitement of the unknown, the anticipation of the laughter that awaits as you step into new chapters of your life.

And so, my fellow explorers, as we take our final bow, let's celebrate the tapestry of thoughts that make us who we are – the beliefs, the contradictions, and the laughter that weaves it all together. The circus tent may fold, but the spirit of cognitive dissonance lives on, reminding us to embrace our human journey with open hearts and a hearty dose of laughter.

Ladies and gentlemen, the stage is cleared, the lights dim, and the audience fades into memory. But the wisdom gained, the laughter shared, and the spirit of cognitive dissonance remain etched in the annals of our minds. So, take a bow, my friends, for you've journeyed through the greatest comedy show of all – the brilliant, bewildering, and utterly enchanting comedy of being human. The final curtain may fall, but the encore of life's laughter is a never-ending symphony that plays on, forever and always.

Chapter 9
A Never-Ending Comedy
The Laughter Continues

Greetings, chucklers and chortlers, as we gather for an encore that promises to tickle your funny bone and expand your mental horizons! In this bonus chapter, we're diving into the never-ending comedy that is life itself, exploring how cognitive dissonance evolves, adapts, and keeps us laughing even as the curtain closes on this book. So, fasten your seatbelts, my friends, because the roller coaster of hilarity is far from over!

The Comedy Continuum
From Beliefs to Enlightenment and Everything In Between
Imagine life as a cosmic amusement park, where each belief you hold is a ticket to a unique ride. There's the "Believe in Santa Claus" coaster, the "Chocolate Cake is a Salad" merry-go-round, and the "Unicorn Whisperer" tunnel of love. But wait, there's also the "I Refuse to Believe I Snore" bumper cars and the "Procrastination is a Virtue"

Ferris wheel.

Cue cognitive dissonance, sporting a flashy jacket and a top hat, leading you through the circus of existence. On one hand, there's the temptation to board only the rides that align with your current beliefs. On the other hand, there's the exhilarating thrill of stepping onto the roller coaster of questioning, the merry-go-round of curiosity, and the bumper cars of self-awareness.

As you navigate this amusement park of life, cognitive dissonance becomes your tour guide, encouraging you to explore all the rides – from the mind-boggling to the sidesplitting. And as you giggle your way through the twists and turns, you realize that enlightenment isn't a fixed destination but a continuous journey fueled by the laughter of self-discovery.

The Evolution of Absurdity
From Bananas in Pyjamas to Quantum Physics

Imagine the history of human thought as a whimsical parade, with each era marching to the beat of its own peculiar drum. There's the "Bananas in Pyjamas" float of childhood innocence, followed by the "Socks with Sandals" float of adolescent rebellion. And let's not forget the "Cat Videos and Dancing Babies" float of internet culture.

Cue cognitive dissonance, riding on the float of time, dressed in a cape

of curiosity and a crown of contemplation. On one hand, there's the temptation to dismiss older beliefs as quaint and outdated. On the other hand, there's the recognition that every era's absurdity adds to the rich tapestry of human experience.

As you watch this parade of thought march by, cognitive dissonance becomes your historian, reminding you that while ideas may change and evolve, the laughter that emerges from our beliefs is a constant companion on our journey through time. The absurdity of yesterday becomes the humor of today, and the mysteries of tomorrow will undoubtedly give rise to even more delightful chuckles.

Laughter as a Bridge
Building Connections Through Cognitive Play

Imagine laughter as the ultimate bridge that connects minds, transcending language barriers, cultural differences, and even the most impenetrable walls of cognitive dissonance. You share a chuckle over a pun, a guffaw at a meme, and suddenly, the gaps between beliefs seem less like chasms and more like footbridges.

Cue cognitive dissonance, now wearing a diplomat's sash and carrying a peace pipe made of punchlines. On one hand, there's the tendency to view differing beliefs as barriers. On the other hand, there's the realization that laughter is a universal language that unites us all in the grand comedy of being human.

As you engage in laughter-induced diplomacy, cognitive dissonance becomes your peacemaker, reminding you that while our beliefs may diverge, the laughter that springs from our minds is a powerful force that can bridge even the widest gaps. And as you share a smile with someone from a different corner of the world, you realize that cognitive dissonance doesn't have to be a wall – it can be a door to connection, understanding, and shared hilarity.

The Grand Encore
A Standing Ovation for the Future

Ladies and gentlemen, as we prepare for the grand encore of our journey through cognitive dissonance, let's remember that the laughter, the learning, and the sheer joy of embracing our quirks are not bound by the pages of this book. The circus tent of the mind remains open, the trapeze of thoughts continues to swing, and the audience of existence eagerly awaits the next act.

Cue cognitive dissonance, now resplendent in a tuxedo and a sparkly bow tie, taking a final bow alongside you. On one hand, there's the sense of completion as we close this chapter. On the other hand, there's the excitement of the future, the promise of new insights, and the untold punchlines that lie ahead.

As the curtain rises on the grand encore, let's celebrate the ongoing comedy of life – the giggles, the snorts, and the belly laughs that

punctuate our days. Our minds are perpetual stages, our thoughts are the performers, and cognitive dissonance is the orchestra conductor that keeps the laughter flowing. So, raise your mental champagne glasses, my friends, and let's toast to the never-ending comedy show of existence. The spotlight may shift, the acts may change, but the laughter echoes on, forever and always.

Appendix
The Great Library of Quirks and Quandaries

Greetings, dear readers, and welcome to the Great Library of Quirks and Quandaries! In this hallowed hall of cognitive curiosities, we've compiled a treasure trove of amusing anecdotes, quirky quotes, and mind-boggling factoids that will tickle your funny bone and expand your mental horizons. Consider this your backstage pass to the inner workings of cognitive dissonance, where laughter and learning dance in a merry jig.

Section 1: "Did I Just Say That?"
Quirky Quotes and Belief Bloopers

Prepare to be entertained and enlightened as we present a collection of quotes that showcase the comedic dance of cognitive dissonance in all its glory. From celebrities to historical figures, these words of wisdom (or folly) will leave you chuckling and scratching your head simultaneously.

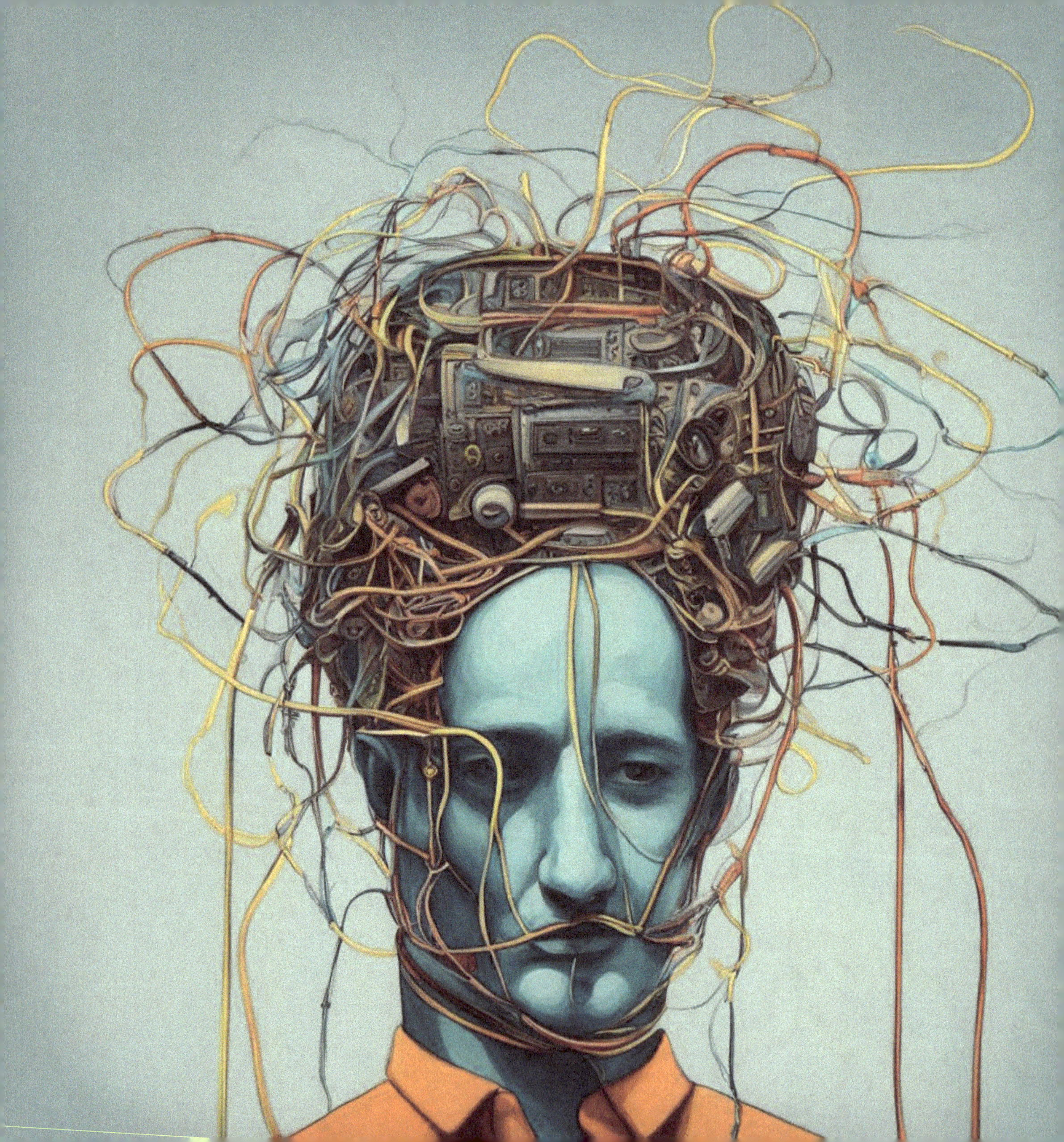

1. "I'm not a vegetarian because I love animals. I'm a vegetarian because I hate plants." - A. Whitney Brown

2. "If it weren't for electricity, we'd all be watching television by candlelight." - George Gobel

3. "I am not young enough to know everything." - Oscar Wilde

4. "Time flies like an arrow; fruit flies like a banana." - Groucho Marx

5. "I'm writing a book. I've got the page numbers done." - Steven Wright

Section 2: "The Factoids That Make You Go Hmmm" Quirky Facts and Mind-Bending Oddities

Hold onto your thinking caps as we dive into a realm of facts that'll make your eyebrows rise and your jaw drop. From historical oddities to bizarre tidbits, these mind-bending factoids will have you questioning the universe and laughing all the way.

1. Honey never spoils. Archaeologists have discovered pots of honey in ancient Egyptian tombs that are over 3,000 years old and still perfectly edible. Now that's what we call eternal sweetness!

2. The shortest war in history lasted just 38 to 45 minutes. It took place

between Britain and Zanzibar in 1896. It probably took them longer to prepare for the battle than to actually fight it!

3. A group of flamingos is called a "flamboyance." So, next time you see a group of these elegant birds, you can marvel at the flamboyant spectacle they create.

4. Cows have best friends. Studies have shown that cows form close friendships and can become stressed when separated from their favorite bovine buddies. Awww, it's a moo-tiful example of social bonding!

5. The national animal of Scotland is the unicorn. Yes, you read that correctly. The mythical creature known for its horn and magical powers holds a special place in Scottish lore.

Section 3: "The Top 10 Beliefs That Make You Raise an Eyebrow"
Absurd Beliefs from Around the World

Get ready to embark on a whirlwind tour of the most eyebrow-raising beliefs from various cultures. From superstitious beliefs to downright wacky notions, these entries will make you marvel at the colorful tapestry of human thought.

1. In Japan, it's considered bad luck to trim your nails at night. Doing

so is believed to bring death to your parents. Better book that manicure appointment for daytime!

2. In Finland, it's believed that if you kill a spider, it will bring rain on your wedding day. Looks like spiders are the original rainmakers!

3. In India, there's a belief that if you sneeze before leaving the house, it's a bad omen and you should delay your journey. Looks like allergies might just save you from a questionable decision!

4. In Iceland, many people believe in the existence of "hidden people" or elves. Some even consult elves before building new structures to ensure they won't disturb these mythical neighbors.

5. In Nigeria, it's believed that if a pregnant woman eats snails, her child will be slow-witted. Looks like snails are the original brain food – but maybe not in the way you'd expect!

And there you have it, dear readers, the treasure trove of oddities, quotes, and beliefs that add a splash of color to the grand tapestry of cognitive dissonance. Remember, while laughter is our guide through the maze of absurdity, it's the wisdom gained that makes the journey truly unforgettable. So, keep your curiosity alive, your funny bone well-tickled, and may your cognitive dissonance forever lead you to the delightful dance of laughter and self-discovery. The library doors are always open, and the laughs are yours to cherish, forever and always.

Acknowledgments
The Laughter Brigade
and Circus of Support

Ladies and gentlemen, jesters and jokers, it's time to roll out the red carpet of gratitude and raise the curtain on the acknowledgment section – the backstage VIP lounge where we give a standing ovation to all those who made this book a reality. From the clowns to the acrobats, the tightrope walkers to the lion tamers, we extend our heartfelt thanks to the cast and crew who brought this comical carnival of cognitive dissonance to life.

The Side-Splitting Supporters
A Round of Applause

First and foremost, we must tip our hats to the unsung heroes who provided a symphony of support during the creation of this whimsical wonder. To the baristas who kept us caffeinated, the delivery drivers who fed our midnight cravings for inspiration, and the WiFi signals that miraculously remained strong during the most crucial writing moments – your contributions may have been unintentional, but they were certainly integral!

The Comedic Catalysts
A Troupe of Inspiring Souls

To the comedians, both famous and obscure, whose witty observations and uproarious anecdotes set the stage for the humor in these pages – you are the true unsung heroes of this carnival. Your ability to find laughter in the everyday and absurd has been the driving force behind this endeavor. Consider this book your honorary backstage pass – please, help yourself to the virtual cotton candy!

The Brainy Backstage Crew
Lights, Laughter, Action!

Behind every great comedy show is a dedicated crew ensuring the lights shine, the sets are stunning, and the punchlines land with precision. To the editors who caught typos before they could pull a pratfall, the designers who turned our words into visual spectacles, and the proofreaders who wielded their red pens like maestros conducting a symphony – your behind-the-scenes magic is what makes this circus shine.

The Audience of Supportive Souls
A Roaring Round of Cheers

To the friends, family, and readers who journeyed alongside us, offering encouragement, enthusiasm, and perhaps a helpful chuckle or two – your cheers from the audience have been the wind beneath our wings (or should we say, the laughter in our sails?). Your willingness to embrace the comedy of cognitive dissonance is a testament to the curious and open-hearted nature of the human spirit.

The Ringleaders of Wisdom
Those Who Inspire and Illuminate

To the thinkers, philosophers, and scholars who have explored the realms of human thought, shedding light on the fascinating dance of cognitive dissonance – your words have been our guiding stars in this vast galaxy of ideas. Your dedication to unraveling the mysteries of the mind has paved the way for the laughter and wisdom shared within these pages.

The Ringmaster of Life
Gratitude Beyond Words

Finally, a standing ovation to life itself – the ultimate circus that has gifted us with the ability to ponder, question, and laugh uproariously at our own absurdities. From the whirlwind of thoughts to the kaleidoscope of beliefs, you have provided us with the canvas on which to paint our cognitive acrobatics. Your grand performance continues to be a source of wonder and joy.

And there you have it, dear readers, the heartwarming, side-splitting acknowledgment section that gives a well-deserved round of applause to all who have contributed to this circus of cognitive dissonance. As the laughter echoes on and the curtain falls, remember that you are an integral part of this grand spectacle. So, keep your sense of humor alive, your mind open to new possibilities, and may your journey through the laughter-filled landscapes of life be endlessly entertaining and enlightening. Bravo, dear friends, and thank you for being part of the greatest show on Earth!

9 798860 308800